21ST CENTURY SCIENCE

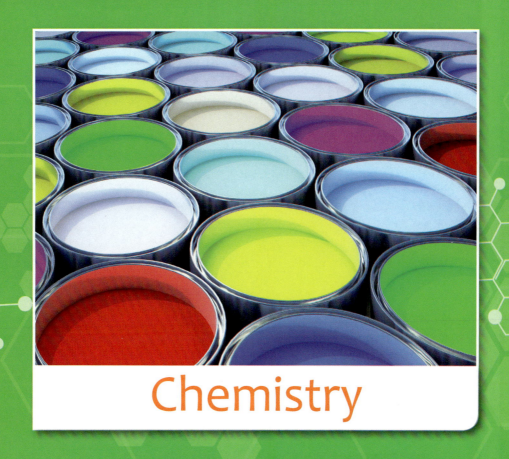

Chemistry

Tom Jackson and Katie Gillespie

LIGHTBOX

Go to
www.openlightbox.com
and enter this book's unique code.

ACCESS CODE

LBQ67768

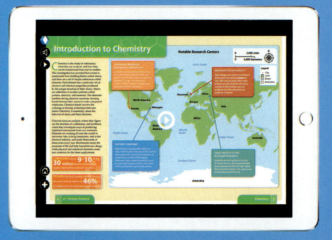

Lightbox is an all-inclusive digital solution for the teaching and learning of curriculum topics in an original, groundbreaking way. Lightbox is based on National Curriculum Standards.

STANDARD FEATURES OF LIGHTBOX

 AUDIO High-quality narration using text-to-speech system

 WEBLINKS Curated links to external, child-safe resources

 INTERACTIVE MAPS Interactive maps and aerial satellite imagery

 VIDEOS Embedded high-definition video clips

 SLIDESHOWS Pictorial overviews of key concepts

 QUIZZES Ten multiple choice questions that are automatically graded and emailed for teacher assessment

ACTIVITIES Printable PDFs that can be emailed and graded

TRANSPARENCIES Step-by-step layering of maps, diagrams, charts, and timelines

 KEY WORDS Matching key concepts to their definitions

 MORE Extra information and details on the subject

 FIRST HAND Letters, diaries, and other primary sources

 DOCS Speeches, newspaper articles, and other historical documents

Copyright © 2018 Smartbook Media Inc. All rights reserved.

2 **21st Century Science**

Contents

2	Access Lightbox Student Edition
4	Introduction to Chemistry
6	Atoms and Elements
8	Compounds and Mixtures
10	Bonds
12	Chemical Reactions
14	Acids, Bases, and Salts
16	Combustion and Fuel
18	Photochemistry
20	Electricity and Chemistry
22	Making Acids and Bases
24	Organic Compounds
26	Polymers
28	Plastics
30	Vital Raw Materials
32	Living Chemistry
34	The Chemical Industry
36	Medical Drugs
38	Chemistry in Food and Agriculture
40	Chemistry in Nature
42	A Cleaner Environment
44	Timeline of Innovations in Chemistry
45	Quiz
46	Key Words
47	Index
48	Log onto www.openlightbox.com

EXTENSION ACTIVITY

Preparing an Annotated Bibliography

Students will create an annotated bibliography comprised of the most useful resources they have identified throughout their research of a scientific discovery. The annotated bibliography will include a variety of types and formats (books, articles, websites, films, government documents) and a summary of each source. An exemplary annotated bibliography will meet the following criteria.

- Sources are credible, relevant to the topic, and are scholarly materials
- Annotations contain clear, complete summaries
- Main points are summarized, including evidence in support of the main point and examples
- All annotations contain evidence of objective evaluation criteria, including author's credentials, accuracy of materials, objectivity, and strengths or weaknesses
- All annotations contain an assessment of the usefulness of the source and the student's reaction to the source. Agree or disagree? Helpful or not, and why? Did the source offer a unique contribution?
- Annotations contain no spelling or grammatical errors
- Annotations are informative
- Any quotations within summaries are properly cited
- All citations are correct in format and include all necessary elements (author or creator's name, date of publication, title, and title of the source or publisher)

Introduction to Chemistry

Chemistry is the study of substances, what they are made of, and how they can be transformed from one to another. This investigation has revealed that nature is constructed from building blocks called atoms, and there are a set of simple substances called elements. Each element has a particular set of physical and chemical properties produced by the unique structure of their atoms. Atoms are collections of smaller particles called protons, electrons, and neutrons. The elements combine during chemical reactions, forming bonds between their atoms to make compound substances. Chemical bonds involve the exchange or sharing of electrons between atoms. Chemistry is essentially about the behavior of atoms and their electrons.

Chemists focus on analysis, where they figure out the structure of a substance, and synthesis, where they investigate ways of producing important compounds from raw materials. Chemists are working all over the world in university labs, at drug companies, and in the chemical industry, and make thousands of discoveries every year. Biochemists study the processes of life and help formulate new drugs, while physical and industrial chemists create new materials for the latest applications.

COMPOUNDS About **9** in **10** of the **30 million** known compounds are organic, meaning they are based on carbon.

OXYGEN is the most common element found on the surface of Earth, making up **46%** of the weight of all rocks and other natural materials.

LAWRENCE BERKELEY NATIONAL LABORATORY

Generally known as the Berkeley Lab, this Californian research center was where chemists first made an artificial element in 1936. They have since made 14 other elements there, more than at any other laboratory.

DUPONT COMPANY

Beginning as a gunpowder factory in 1802, DuPont grew into one of the world's most important chemical companies. Its researchers, based in Wilmington, Delaware, have created chemicals such as nylon and neoprene fabric, non-stick teflon, and kevlar used in body armor.

Notable Research Centers

MANCHESTER UNIVERSITY
This college was where researchers discovered the atomic **nucleus** in 1911. This was 110 years after John Dalton, an early chemist who also worked in Manchester, set out evidence that the elements are made up of atoms.

JOINT INSTITUTE FOR NUCLEAR RESEARCH
Scientists at this facility, in the city of Dubna, Russia, discovered the last seven elements in the Periodic Table. They included element 118, oganesson, the heaviest element of all.

TEACHER NOTES

Google Maps
Sites of Notable Research Centers
Explore the sites of several important scientific locations using street view.

1. What do these sites all have in common with each other? Why are these similarities significant?
2. Why do you think that scientists and researchers at these particular sites have been so successful in their scientific work? How would their level of success be affected if they were working in other locations instead?
3. What factors have contributed to the scientific discoveries and developments made at these sites? What changes or improvements can you think of that might increase the chances of more scientific breakthroughs at these sites in the future?

▶ Video
Introduction to Chemistry with Hank
Explore the basics of chemistry by watching this video introducing the topic.

1. What is the purpose of this video? Is it effective in achieving this purpose? Explain your answer.
2. What is the difference between an ion and an atom?
3. What are the four different kinds of orbitals?

Chemistry | 5

Atoms and Elements

A scanning tunneling microscope uses a fine needle to detect atoms.

Modern chemistry is understood in terms of the behavior of atoms, which transform into compounds by breaking and then making bonds during chemical reactions. However, a single **atom** if far too small to observe directly. The invention of the scanning tunneling microscope in the 1980s allowed chemists to detect the spaces occupied by single atoms, but the behaviors of their electrons and other particles are understood purely by indirect evidence.

Despite being central to the understanding of modern chemistry, the atom is actually a very old idea. The ancient Greeks believed that atoms were particles that cannot be subdivided further, and named them "atomos," meaning "indivisible." In 1801, Dalton showed that the behaviors of gases proved that all substances were made of atoms. A century later, scientists began to discover three smaller particles inside atoms. These subatomic particles are positively charged protons, negatively charged electrons, and neutrons, which are neutral. The center, or **nucleus**, of atoms contains neutrons and protons, and has a positive charge. The electrons move around the nucleus and are held in place by the attraction of the positive charge of the protons in the nucleus.

Elements

An element is a substance that cannot be broken down into a set of simpler substances. Common examples of elements are carbon, gold, and iron. Water is a compound because it is built from atoms of two elements, oxygen and hydrogen. Each of the 118 elements has a unique number of protons, called the **atomic number**, and a corresponding equal number of electrons in their atoms. The number of neutrons may vary, forming a different version, or isotope, of an element's atoms.

The properties of an element are based in the arrangement of their electrons. These fill concentric shells, or **orbitals**, around the nucleus. When one shell is filled, the electrons start filling the next layer further out. Almost all elements have atoms with outer shells that have empty spaces for more electrons. Chemical reactions occur as atoms attempt to fill their outer electron shells and so become more structurally stable. The precise configuration of electrons tells a chemist how an element will react.

The Periodic Table

Chemists used the Periodic Table to predict how elements behave. In the table, elements are arranged in order of atomic number. The elements with similar atomic structures—and similar properties—appear at regular, or periodic, intervals. These are arranged in columns, or groups. Members of a group have the same number of electrons in their outer shells. Members of a row, known as a period, have atoms with the same number of electron shells.

TEACHER NOTES

🌐 **Weblink**

Dynamic Periodic Table
Review the periodic table to learn more about the elements.

1. How does this dynamic periodic table differ from a static periodic table? What advantages does this provide? Why?
2. Who might benefit from using a dynamic periodic table such as this one? In what ways? Give specific examples.

Russian Dmitri Mendeleev created the first Periodic Table in 1869.

EXTENSION ACTIVITY

Create a Scientific Poster

Students will create a scientific poster exploring the topic of compounds and mixtures. An exemplary poster will meet the following criteria.

- The poster has a title that suggests the chosen topic or theme
- The poster presents relevant and accurate information about the topic or theme
- The format of the poster is appropriate to the content, purpose, and audience for which it was designed
- Visuals such as pictures, photographs, charts, tables, scientific drawings, or diagrams add to the effectiveness of the poster
- The poster is well organized and the poster elements work well together
- The use of appropriate graphic design tools, space, color, texture, and shape effectively creates an aesthetically pleasing product
- The poster draws attention
- Language chosen for the poster is accurate, informative, and concise

Compounds and Mixtures

There are two ways that substances can come together. They can either combine as compounds or as mixtures. A compound is made up of two or more elements. Their atoms are connected by chemical bonds to form molecules. The atoms can only be separated again by breaking these bonds in a **chemical reaction.** For example, water (H_2O) is one of the most abundant compounds on Earth's surface. The hydrogen (H) and oxygen (O) atoms cannot be separated by a physical process, such as filtering, because water is a single, cohesive substance.

The only way to purify the elemental constituents of water is to add energy, which will break the bonds that link them. By contrast, the ingredients of a mixture are not chemically bonded. They are only physically mixed and can be separated by a physical process, such as sorting, filtering, or distillation.

Types of mixture

One example of a mixture can be found in a typical trash can. It probably contains a variety of different substances, such as glass, paper, plastic, and metal, which although thoroughly mixed have no link. It is a relatively simple task to separate the different components. A bowl of fruit in an example of a heterogeneous mixture, which means the different materials are unevenly mixed. Each ingredient is easily identified among the others, and so is easily removed. Other kinds of mixtures are homogeneous, where the ingredients are more evenly mixed and cannot be told apart.

Solvents and solutes

An everyday example of a homogeneous mixture is a drink, such as a cup of coffee, tea, or a fizzy soda. In this mixture, certain compounds—the sugar, flavors, and gases—

Cloud is an aerosol mixture of water droplets mixed with air.

Solid sugar splits into individual molecules as it dissolves in water, such as in coffee or tea.

8 | 21st Century Science

are dissolved in a liquid. The liquid, in these cases water, is called the **solvent**. The other substances, known as the **solutes**, are evenly spread through the solvent and effectively disappear, although the color may change. This kind of mixture is called a solution. The molecular structure of water makes it an excellent solvent. Water is known as the "universal solvent" because so many substances, including the salt in seawater, can be dissolved in it.

Separating solvents and solutes is more complex than sorting trash. To extract sugar from tea, the water can be heated so it boils away. The sugar does not boil at the same temperature as the water and so is left behind. This method of separation is known as evaporation. If one wanted to make pure water from the tea, a similar technique could be used. However, the water vapor released is then collected and cooled down so it turns back into liquid water. This method of separation is known as distillation.

Emulsions

Many people add milk or cream to their coffee and tea. Milk is a mixture made of water and oily fats. This mixture is homogeneous, which means it is not possible to see where the water ends and the fat begins. However, it is not a solution, but a type of mixture called an **emulsion**. Tiny droplets of liquid fat are floating in the water—or tea/coffee solution. These droplets are considerably larger than the particles of dissolved solutes, and if left perfectly still for a long time, the two materials will gradually separate out. In this example, the milk will rise to the surface, making a creamy layer on top. Stirring will mix them again.

It is common for foods that mix water and fats, such as salad dressing, in this way to use chemicals called emulsifiers. These form links between the water and fat, slowing their separation. The natural emulsifier lecithin, which is found in egg yolks, is often used in foods.

TEACHER NOTES

▶ Video

Dissociation of salt
Learn more about dissociation of salt by watching this video.

1. How are sodium chloride crystals held together?
2. What happens when a crystal of sodium chloride is placed into water?

🌐 Weblink

Compounds and mixtures
Review the article to discover more about compounds and mixtures.

1. Compare and contrast the properties of compounds and mixtures. How are they similar? How are they different?
2. What are five ways of separating the different substances in mixtures? Explain each method and give an example of when each might be used that does not appear in the article.

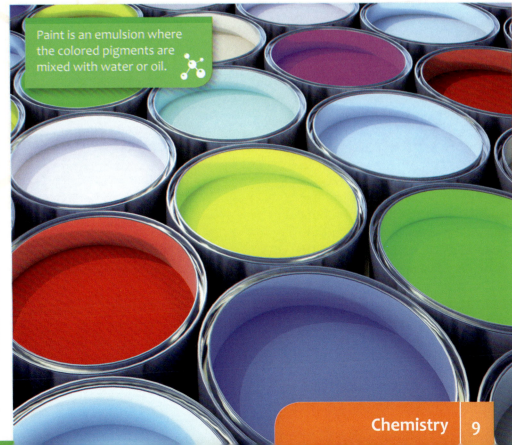

Paint is an emulsion where the colored pigments are mixed with water or oil.

Chemistry

Ionic compounds such as salt are often soluble in water. The water molecules are able to split up the ions.

Bonds

Electrons are the smallest atomic particles. They are more than 1,800 times smaller than neutrons or protons, but they are used by atoms to form bonds during chemical reactions and determine the chemical properties of elements.

How atoms join

Atoms are always seeking stability. Those that have an incomplete outer shell of electrons try to fill them by partnering with other atoms in a process that bonds them together. Elements, such as helium and argon, which have a full outer shell of electrons, do not form bonds with other atoms. These elements are known as the **"noble" gases** because they do not mix with "common" elements.

Ionic bond

There are two main types of atomic bond called ionic and covalent. In an ionic bond, an atom with a few outer electrons gives them away, shedding that incomplete outer shell, leaving a full one underneath. Losing electrons converts the atom into a positively charged ion. For example, sodium (Na) loses one outer electron to become the sodium **ion** (Na$^+$). Chlorine (Cl) has just one empty space in its outer shell and takes the electron shed by the sodium to become a negatively charged chloride ion (Cl$^-$). Both ions now have a full outer shell, and are attracted together by the opposite charges. This attraction creates an ionic bond between them, forming a molecule of sodium chloride (NaCl), otherwise known as common salt. Ionic molecules are always electrically neutral, and several positive and negative ions can bond together to achieve this.

Covalent bond

Ionic bonds generally form between metals, which have a few outer electrons, and non-metals, which have nearly full outer shells. Non-metal atoms bond covalently, where they share—not swap— electrons to fill their outer shells. Two or more atoms come together so their outer shells merge. Outer electrons from the atoms are attracted to the nuclei at the center of all atoms, and these forces hold the atoms together as a covalent molecule. Common covalent molecules include water and methane.

Dipole Attraction

Electrons in covalent bonds are not always shared equally between the atoms. Unequal sharing, as in a molecule of water, creates a **dipole**, where there is a slight positive charge at one end, or pole, and a corresponding negative charge at the other end of the molecule. The dipole is there because oxygen pulls on the shared electrons more strongly than the hydrogen atoms. The charged poles can link neighboring molecules together. In the case of water, its polar molecule results in a particularly strong form of dipole–dipole attraction, known as a **hydrogen bond**. Although it is weak compared with normal chemical bonds, this bond has significant effects. The bonds make the boiling point of water much higher than similar compounds, such as hydrogen sulfide (H_2S). More energy is needed to break the hydrogen bonds and separate the water molecules to make them into a gas. Without this effect, water would not be a liquid on Earth. Hydrogen bonding also makes water molecules spread out a little as they freeze into solid ice. This makes ice less dense than water, so it floats on warmer water. Other solid compounds are almost universally denser than their liquid forms.

TEACHER NOTES

🔷 Transparency
Covalent Molecules
Examine the diagram and research online to learn more about covalent molecules.

1. Describe in your own words what is happening in the diagram.
2. What is a covalent molecule? How do covalent bonds form?
3. Which is the simplest covalent molecule? How do you find the charge of a covalent molecule?

🌐 Weblink
Metallic Bonding
Review the article to find out how the metallic bond arises and why its strength varies from metal to metal.

1. What is a metallic bond? Explain in your own words using specific examples.
2. Which factors increase the strength of the bond between magnesium and sodium?
3. Why do transition metals tend to have particularly high melting points and boiling points?

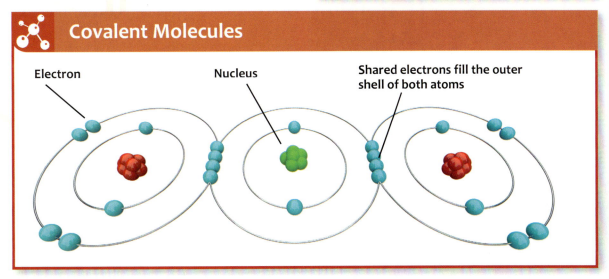

Covalent Molecules

Electron — Nucleus — Shared electrons fill the outer shell of both atoms

Chemistry | 11

EXTENSION ACTIVITY

Analyzing a Scientific Biography

Students will research the life of a scientific figure and present their findings. An exemplary biographical analysis will meet the following criteria.

- Illustrates strong knowledge of the subject
- Identifies the author of the biography
- Describes why the subject of the biography is important
- Contains information about the time and place in which the subject was born
- Lists important events in the subject's life
- Explains how events in the subject's life impacted him or her
- Makes inferences about the subject, based on events in his or her life
- Explains how the subject influenced the world while he or she lived
- Researches the cultural and historical context of the subject's life
- Examines the effect that the subject has had on the modern world
- Supplements information from the biography with independent research
- Organizes the analysis in a logical, effective manner
- Uses correct spelling, grammar, and punctuation
- Cites all sources used in the analysis

Chemical Reactions

A chemical reaction occurs when the bonds between atoms break apart and reform in a different combination. As a result, the starting materials, known as the **reactants**—these could be pure elements, compounds, or a mixture of both—are converted into new materials, known as the products. Chemists investigate the causes of chemical reactions and seek to control them.

Reactivity

Atoms seek stability, which means having a complete outer shell of electrons. They do this by forming bonds with other atoms. The elements of some atoms are more likely to get involved in reactions than others, depending on how easy it is for them to achieve a stable state. For example, sodium only has to lose one electron to become stable, but magnesium has to shed two electrons. Therefore, sodium is more likely to react and form bonds than magnesium. Similarly, chlorine only needs to gain one electron to become stable, but carbon needs to add four. Therefore, chlorine is more reactive than carbon.

Activation energy

All reactions need a supply of **energy**, known as activation energy, to stretch and break bonds in the reactants, and start the reaction. The amount of energy needed to break a particular bond is known as its bond energy. The stronger the bond, the more difficult it is to break, and therefore the link is said to have a high bond energy.

Releasing heat

Energy is needed to make chemical bonds as well as break them. There is almost always a mismatch between the energy needed to break up the reactants and the energy required to form the products. Reactions such as cell

When rockets propellants react, they release much more energy than they take in.

12 | 21st Century Science

respiration, acid–base neutralization, and combustion, such as the burning of a campfire or a fireworks display, result in unused energy being released as heat and light. This is because it takes less energy to make the products of the reaction than it does to break up the reactant. These reactions are exothermic reactions because they give out energy.

Reactions such as photosynthesis, which is the reaction sequence by which plants convert the energy of sunlight into food, and electrolysis, a process that uses electricity to break up compounds, need more energy to create the products than is used to break down the reactants. As a result, they need a constant input of energy to make them go forward, or in some cases, the reaction will take energy from the surroundings, making the temperature drop. These types of reactions are known as endothermic reactions. They draw in heat, or other forms of energy.

Using reactions

As long ago as 1874, the science-fiction writer Jules Verne predicted that the hydrogen and oxygen in water would one day be employed as a fuel. The reaction of oxygen and hydrogen, where they combine to produce water, is highly explosive—and exothermic. That huge release of energy is used to power the most powerful rocket engines, such as the ones used by large spacecraft.

Catalysts

Activation energy can be achieved by increasing temperature and pressure. The rate at which the reaction then occurs can be boosted by increasing the concentration of the reactants and mixing them more thoroughly. Another way is to use a catalyst. **Catalysts** are substances that speed up the rate of a reaction by lowering their activation energy. The catalyst takes part in the reaction in some way but is not permanently changed by it.

Names and Formulas

In the early years of chemistry, researchers gave names to the newly discovered elements. For several decades, no one could agree on what names to use. For example, nitrogen was originally known as "azote," while oxygen was "dephlogisticated air." Compounds also had confusing common names. Carbon dioxide was originally called "chaos of wood." Eventually, accepted names for new substances were adopted, but a language barrier persisted with more familiar elements, such as iron, carbon, and sulfur, all being called different things in different countries. In the early 1800s, a Swedish scientist called Jöns Jacob Berzelius suggested identifying elements using an international set of symbols, made up of one or two letters. This eventually became the system used by modern chemists. Berzelius also proposed representing compounds as formulas of these symbols. The formula for water shows that a water molecule has two hydrogen (H) atoms for every one oxygen (O) atom.

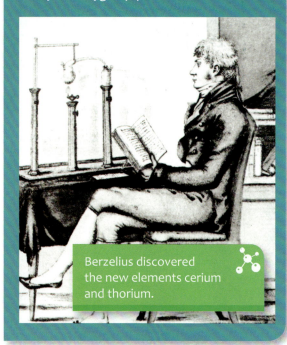

Berzelius discovered the new elements cerium and thorium.

TEACHER NOTES

More
Names and Formulas
Review how Berzelius' formulas were used to simplify chemical reactions using equations.

1. What is the purpose of a chemical equation? Explain the advantages in your own words.
2. What kinds of information can be obtained from a balanced equation? What limitations do they have?
3. Where is the number of atoms of the reactants shown in a chemical equation? Where is the number of atoms of the products shown in a chemical equation?

Video
Nomenclature - Crash Course Chemistry #44
Learn more about International Union of Pure and Applied Chemistry (IUPAC), prefixes, suffixes, ranking, numbers for carbon chains, and cis or trans double bonds by watching this video.

1. Explain in your own words the process of naming a chemical.
2. What is the parent functional group? How is it determined?

Chemistry | 13

EXTENSION ACTIVITY

Conduct a Scientific Experiment

Students will research and conduct a scientific experiment. An exemplary experiment will meet the following criteria.

- Background research is thorough, specific, and has many examples
- All ideas are clearly explained
- History, biology, and pros and cons are fully addressed
- Scientific problem is new, meaningful, and well researched
- Hypothesis is clearly stated in the "If…then" format
- Scientific procedure is detailed, appropriate, and thorough
- Steps of procedure are listed and sequential
- All materials used are listed
- Potential safety issues have been addressed
- Variables have been identified
- Controls are appropriate, in place, and explained
- Sample size is appropriate and explained

Acids, Bases, and Salts

Acids are compounds that contain hydrogen and dissolve in water to release hydrogen ions. Since a hydrogen ion is a hydrogen atom that has lost its electron, and therefore consists of just one proton, acids are also known as proton donors. When they are dissolved in water, acids act as good electrolytes, which means they allow an electric current to run through the water. The charge of the current is not carried by electrons, as is normally the case, but by the positively charged hydrogen ions.

Acid chemistry

The strongest acids are highly corrosive substances, and accordingly, they must be handled with great care. Other acids, such as vinegar and citric acid, are much less corrosive. They can be used to add flavor to foods with their sour, sharp taste. The protons in acids are readily accepted during reactions by other chemicals called bases. A base is a good proton acceptor because it contains oxide (O^{2-}) or hydroxide (OH^-) ions. Many bases cannot be dissolved in water, but those that can are known as alkalis. Indigestion tablets and cleaners for household drains are everyday examples of basic chemicals. Caustic soda (sodium hydroxide, NaOH) and lime (calcium oxide, CaO) are powerful bases used in industrial processes.

Neutralization

When acids and bases are mixed, they combine in a reaction known as neutralization to form an ionic compound, called a salt, and water. For example, hydrochloric acid (HCl) neutralizes sodium hydroxide to

Most metals produce hydrogen bubbles when reacting with acids, but copper does not.

Volcanic springs contain strong acids derived from dissolved minerals.

produce common salt (sodium chloride) and water. Neutralization reactions are always exothermic. They release heat as the reaction takes place. A salt is a neutral compound, meaning it is neither acidic or basic.

Making salts

Other acid reactions also produce a salt. For example, an acid reacts with a carbonate, a compound containing an ion built from carbon and oxygen, to produce a salt, water, and carbon dioxide (CO_2). This is the reaction that occurs when vinegar, the acid, is added to baking powder, the base, in volcano models. The resulting carbon dioxide creates the "lava" foam. When pure metals—at least more reactive types—are added to an acid, the reaction produces a salt and pure hydrogen gas. This reaction was used to isolate the first supplies of hydrogen gas—then an unknown "inflammable air"—by English chemist Henry Cavendish in 1766.

The pH Scale

The strength of an acid or base is measured using the pH, or "potential hydrogen", scale. A substance's pH shows its concentration of hydrogen ions. Neutral substances, such as water, have a pH of 7, which means there is one hydrogen ion for every 10 million (10^7) water molecules. An acid has more ions than this and so has a lower pH value. An alkali has even fewer hydrogen ions and so has a pH value that is higher than 7.

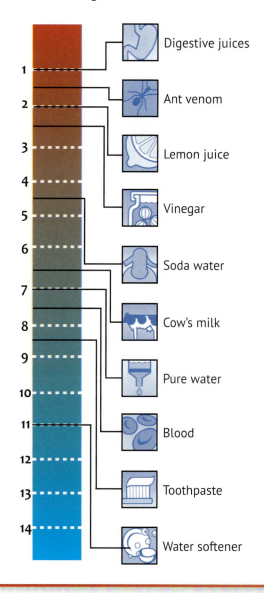

TEACHER NOTES

Transparency

The pH Scale
Examine the diagram and research online to learn more about the pH scale.

1. Explain what is happening at each stage of the diagram.
2. What is the pH value of lemon juice? Is it more or less acidic than vinegar?
3. What is the pH value of toothpaste? Is it more or less basic than cow's milk?

Weblink

Acids, bases, and salts
Review the article to discover more about acids, bases, and salts.

1. What happens when acids react with carbonates? Name the extra product that is made.
2. What happens when alkalis dissolve in water? How does ammonia differ?
3. How many parts does the name of a salt have? What does each part mean? Explain how the names of salts made from hydrochloric acid differ from the names of salts made from sulfuric acid.

Chemistry

Combustion and Fuel

Fuels are compounds that contain stored chemical energy. This energy is released in exothermic reactions where the fuel reacts with oxygen. The energy from fuels is put to work. Living things are fueled by sugars, while **hydrocarbons**, such as oil, gas, and coal, are fuels used to provide the energy to heat houses, run engines, and generate electricity.

Forms of combustion

The reaction that releases energy from fuels is called combustion. The fuel reacts with oxygen—generally present as a component of air but sometimes supplied as a pure gas.

All widely used fuels, such as oil, natural gas, and coal, contain carbon, and so the combustion reaction results in those fuels being converted into carbon dioxide and water.

Combustion is generally a rapid reaction, where heat is released as flames. Respiration, the process used by living cells to release energy from food, is a highly controlled form of combustion that reacts glucose and other sugars with oxygen in several stages to eventually produce water and carbon dioxide. The energy released as a result of this process is used to help an organism live and grow.

Combustion causes $14 billion worth of damage each year in the United States.

Rate of burning

The rate of combustion depends on conditions such as the concentration of oxygen. Air is only about one-fifth oxygen. The rest is mainly inert nitrogen, and fuels burn much faster in pure oxygen. Controlling the concentration of the fuel and the temperature is also important for controlling combustion.

A wax candle does not give out its light until it is given the activation energy it needs from a match or spark. This applies to all fuels. This activation energy is used to break bonds, so that new bonds can start to form. The combustion reaction is exothermic overall, and it provides its own energy once the reaction gets going. As a burning candle demonstrates, the reaction stops when the supply of fuel or oxygen runs out.

Energy from fuel

The amount of energy given off by the combustion of a fuel depends on the number of bonds to be broken and made. This is related to the size of the fuel molecule and the type of bonds involved. For this reason, larger hydrocarbon molecules such as octane (C_8H_{18}), a typical constituent of gasoline, give off more energy per molecule than methane (natural gas, CH_4), which has only one carbon atom. However, setting octane alight requires a larger activation energy. Partly oxidized fuels—including ethanol (C_2H_5OH), the alcohol in alcoholic drinks—are used as alternatives fuels, but they give off even less energy. This is because they already contain O–H bonds in their structure. The energy released during combustion comes from the making of bonds to oxygen, so fuels that already contain oxygen give out less energy when they burn.

Controlling Fire

Understanding the chemical reactions that occur during fires can make it possible to prevent fires from starting and bringing them under control when they do. Fire requires a fuel and oxygen, the reactants, and a source of heat, which provides the activation energy that starts and maintains the reaction. These three elements are often known as the fire triangle, and firefighters will use different methods to remove one of them to put the fire out.

Chemical Explosives

An explosive is a chemical or mixture of chemicals that reacts rapidly releasing gas products and heat energy. In low explosives, such as gunpowder, the rapid reaction results from heat spreading through the substance. High explosives, such as TNT and nitroglycerin, detonate, which means the reaction spreads due to a supersonic pressure wave of gas.

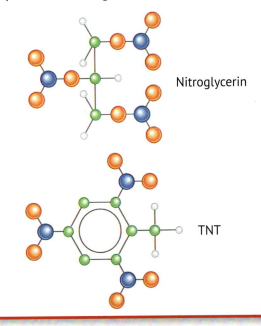

Nitroglycerin

TNT

TEACHER NOTES

More
Controlling Fire
Review the different methods of extinguishing fires.

1. What kinds of fire cannot be put out by water? Why not?
2. How does a dry chemical extinguisher work?
3. What methods may be used to combat larger fires, such as forest fires or bush fires? Are they typically effective? Why or why not?

Transparency
Chemical Explosives
Examine the diagram and research online to learn more about chemical explosives.

1. What is depicted in this diagram? Describe it in your own words.
2. Compare and contrast nitroglycerin and TNT. How are they similar? In what ways are they different?

Chemistry 17

Photochemistry

Most chemical reactions require energy and some reactions get this energy from light. Light carries energy with it as "packets" called photons. The amount of energy in light is indicated by its **wavelength**. High-energy light has a short wavelength, and low-energy light has a long wavelength. Human eyes can detect wavelength, and the brain interprets the differences as color. Red light is lower energy than green, which, in turn, has less energy than blue light.

Every atom and molecule is able to accept, or absorb, the energy of light with certain wavelengths. Everything else bounces off—or is reflected. When an atom or molecule absorbs a photon of light, it adopts an excited state as its energy increases. It can then readily take part in reactions. Some of the best known photochemical reactions take place in photography. Another example is the process of photosynthesis, where plants use light-sensitive chemicals to capture useful energy from sunlight.

Reaction of chlorine and hydrogen

One of the first photochemical reactions to be studied was the action of light on a dry mixture of chlorine and hydrogen gases. The final result of the reaction is the formation of hydrogen chloride, which occurs in a series of stages that make up a chemical chain reaction. First of all, light splits molecules of chlorine (Cl_2) into two chlorine atoms (Cl), each chlorine molecule absorbing one photon of light in the process. Then, each of the highly reactive lone chlorine atoms immediately reacts with a hydrogen molecule (H_2) to produce a hydrogen chloride (HCl) molecule and a free hydrogen atom (H). The free

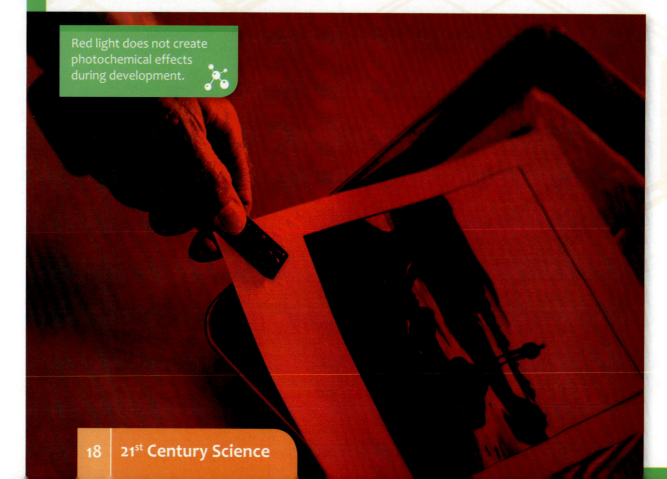

Red light does not create photochemical effects during development.

hydrogen atom reacts with another chlorine molecule to produce more hydrogen chloride and another free chlorine atom. These second and third reactions are what is termed a chain reaction. It may proceed so rapidly as to result in an explosion. The reaction comes to an end when all free chlorine and hydrogen atoms have combined to form hydrogen chloride.

Photography

Until the advent of digital cameras, photographic film was a common application of photochemistry. Images were captured on a thin sheet, or film, of plastic. The film's emulsion, which is the light-sensitive coating on its surface, is made up of grains of silver bromide (AgBr). When a photograph is taken, the film is exposed to light for a fraction of a second. This causes some of the millions of molecules in each silver bromide grain to break down into silver and bromide ions. Areas of the film exposed to light contain large numbers of silver atoms, but unexposed areas do not.

The film is developed into a visible image by using a developer chemical, often hydroquinone. This splits the silver bromide into ions in the areas of the film that are already rich in free silver ions, making a black patch. Regions that have no silver atoms remain white. The result is a negative image in which bright and dark objects are reversed. A positive print is made by imaging the negative using the same process.

The ozone layer

Ozone is a form of oxygen where three atoms make a molecule (O_3) instead of the regular two (O_2). It is formed in a photochemical reaction by the action of high-energy ultraviolet (UV) light. Ozone is dangerous to breathe, but it mostly forms in a layer about 15 miles (25 kilometers) up. This high ozone layer absorbs harmful UV radiation that would otherwise reach Earth's surface.

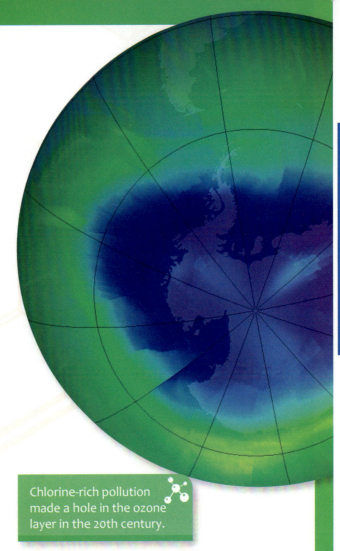

Chlorine-rich pollution made a hole in the ozone layer in the 20th century.

THE FIRST PHOTO was made in **1822** by French inventor Nicéphore Niépce using silver nitrate.

PHOTOSYNTHESIS is less than **2%** efficient. This is enough to produce the necessary sugars to give the plant the energy it needs.

OZONE CONCENTRATION For every **10 million** molecules of gas in the air, **6** are ozone.

TEACHER NOTES

🌐 **Weblink**

Photochemistry
Review the article to discover more about photochemistry.

1. What are the first and second laws of photochemistry? Explain them in your own words.
2. What does the Franck-Condron principle require? Describe the potential events that may then take place.
3. When does a photochemical reaction occur?

Chemistry | 19

EXTENSION ACTIVITY

Write an Abstract

Students will use their library or *Google Scholar* to find a scientific research article or study related to electrochemistry, then write a 300-word abstract. An exemplary abstract will meet the following criteria.

- States the research question or problem that the author is answering
- Indicates the significance of the issue
- Describes and explains methods used by the scientist(s)
- Explains why the methods used by the scientist(s) were appropriate
- Explains why this article or study stands out and how it is different from others
- Clearly states how the article or study advances knowledge about the topic, why it is important, and how it can be used
- Introductory statement is clear, concise, and engaging
- Purpose is clear, concise, and relevant
- Explanation of the findings includes what was expected, discovered, accomplished, collected, and produced
- Clearly states the conclusion
- Conclusion describes how the work contributes to the field
- Writing is appropriate and free from grammatical errors

Electricity and Chemistry

The addition and removal of electrons is one of the key processes in chemical bonding. This is the basis of electrochemistry, in which electrical currents are used to drive chemical reactions by pushing electrons from one substance to another. Electrochemistry is mostly used to purify metals and for electroplating.

Industrial electrochemistry

Electrochemical reactions are carried out in electrochemical cells. These contain an electrolyte, a power supply, a positive **electrode** (anode), which accepts electrons from the electrolyte, and a negative electrode (cathode), which releases electrons. An electrochemical cell works in the opposite way to a battery. In a battery, electricity is produced by a chemical reaction, which is the movement of ions through an electrolyte from one type of electrode to another. In an electrochemical cell, electricity is used to drive a similar chemical reaction in the opposite direction.

Electrolysis is used to manufacture many important chemicals. For example, the electrolysis of brine, a highly concentrated solution of salt, produces three industrial products. These are sodium hydroxide, chlorine, and hydrogen gas. The method involves graphite anodes and a pool of liquid mercury as a cathode. The electrolyte is brine, made up of 25 percent salt dissolved in water. Chlorine ions give an electron to the graphite anode and transform into pure chlorine gas. The sodium ions receive an electron from the cathode, becoming pure metal. The metal dissolves in the mercury, forming an alloy,

Electrolysis splits water into oxygen and hydrogen. Twice as much hydrogen is produced as oxygen.

or metal mixture, called amalgam. The amalgam flows out into another cell, where the sodium is removed by reacting it with water, making sodium hydroxide and hydrogen gas. The purified mercury flows back into the original cell to collect more sodium.

Metal refining

Aluminum is the most common metal in Earth's rocks, but is too reactive and too strongly bonded in its ores to be refined using regular chemical reactions. Therefore, electrolysis must be used. Bauxite, the principle aluminum **ore**, is dissolved in molten cryolite, a naturally occurring aluminum fluoride mineral that acts as an electrolyte. Carbon is used for both the anodes and the cathodes. Aluminum ions

Chromium-plated metals do not rust and stay looking shiny.

TEACHER NOTES

🌐 Weblink
Electrolytic cells and electrolysis
Examine the article to discover more about the decomposition of substances by electric currents.

1. What is thermal diffusion? How does it relate to ionic transport?
2. What happens when an aqueous solution is subjected to electrolysis?
3. Explain how an electrolytic cell is the opposite of a galvanic cell.

gather at the negatively-charged cathode, collect electrons, and become pure molten aluminum, which is drained off. The process consumes a vast amount of electricity, which makes aluminum very expensive to make compared to iron and copper. However, because it does not corrode, pure aluminum objects, such as drink cans, can be easily recycled.

Electroplating
In electroplating, one metal is coated with a fine layer of another. This is done to make objects look more attractive and to prevent corrosion. The object to be plated is used as the cathode, while the anode is made from the plating metal.

Electrolysis is used to purify copper from alloys. The current pulls only copper ions from the alloy.

Chemistry | 21

A sulfuric acid plant uses huge reaction chambers to make the chemical.

Making Acids and Bases

Some economists claim that the amount of sulfuric acid produced by a nation is a good indicator of its economic power. Wealthy countries manufacture a lot of strong acids as a raw material for use in the many areas of their chemical industry. Acids and bases, their opposites, are used in a wide range of industrial processes, such as the manufacture of plastics, fertilizers, and cement.

Sulfuric acid

Sulfuric acid (H_2SO_4) is one of the leading products of the chemical industry, and most of the pure sulfur produced worldwide is used for its manufacture. In the United States, for example, almost twice as much sulfuric acid is produced as any other chemical. Sulfuric acid is one of the strongest known acids, and has a wide range of applications in almost all manufacturing processes. It is commonly used in the manufacture of dyes, paints, paper pulp, explosives, car batteries, and fertilizers. It is also used to make detergents, and in petroleum and metal refining. It is an excellent dehydrating agent, and dissolves metals to form a wide variety of useful industrial compounds.

The starting material for the acid is pure sulfur, most of which is extracted from deposits deep underground. Superheated water, which is hotter than boiling point but compressed to a high pressure to keep it liquid, is pumped into the deposit. The water melts the sulfur, and a hot liquid mixture of molten sulfur and water is pumped back to the surface.

Sulfuric acid is manufactured by the Contact Process. Sulfur is first burned in dry air to form sulfur dioxide (SO_2) gas. The hot SO_2 is reacted with more oxygen at a temperature of about 842° Fahrenheit (450° Celsius) in the presence of a vanadium oxide (V_2O_5) catalyst

Pure sulfur is mined by hand in volcanic regions.

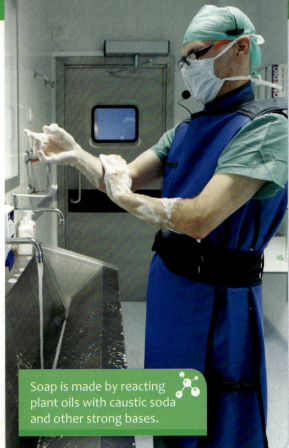

Soap is made by reacting plant oils with caustic soda and other strong bases.

TEACHER NOTES

⊕ Weblink
The chlor-alkali industry
Review the article to find out more about the chlor-alkali industry.

1. What happens if an electric current is passed through a concentrated sodium chloride solution?
2. What are the uses of hydrogen, chlorine, and sodium hydroxide in the chemical industry?

to form sulfur trioxide (SO_3). Sulfuric acid can be formed by reacting the SO_3 with water, but this reaction is very violent and forms a mist of dangerous sulfuric acid droplets that is difficult to absorb. Instead, SO_3 is dissolved in concentrated (98 percent solution) sulfuric acid, where it reacts less violently. The resulting product is oleum ($H_2S_2O_7$), which is a slightly weaker acid that is used in some industrial processes. To make sulfuric acid, the oleum is diluted with water to form concentrated sulfuric acid.

Caustic soda

Among the bases, lye, also known as caustic soda or sodium hydroxide, is one of the most important. It is widely used in processes including the manufacture of soap, paper, detergents, and other chemicals as well as for the production of the artificial fabrics rayon and acetate. Caustic soda is produced in chloralkali plants by the electrolysis of brine.

Electrolysis splits dissolved sodium chloride into pure sodium and chlorine. The sodium later reacts with water to make a solution of caustic soda. Any caustic soda remaining in the mixture crystallizes out and is removed by filtration. The chlorine gas produced is scrubbed clean using sulfuric acid. The gas has many uses, one of which is to make hydrochloric acid, another very important chemical used in refining metals.

GLOBAL PRODUCTION
Every year, the world produces **253 million tons** of sulfuric acid. (230 million tonnes)

CHLORALKALI
The total value of the products made by the chloralkali process is **$70 billion.**

Chemistry 23

EXTENSION ACTIVITY

Analyzing a Scientific Video

Students will watch and assess a video related to a scientific discovery, and write an analysis of the video. An exemplary video analysis will meet the following criteria.

- Identifies the purpose of the video
- Identifies the intended audience of the video
- Identifies the video as a primary or secondary source
- Discusses the scientific and social context of the video
- Describes how the content of the video is presented
- Summarizes the information and opinions presented in the video
- Analyzes the quality of the content presented in the video
- Assesses the effectiveness of the video
- Determines whether the images and graphics used in the video relate to the content
- Determines whether the video is easy to follow and understand
- Gives the analysis a clear and consistent purpose
- Organizes the analysis in a logical, effective manner
- Presents a strong, clear argument about the video
- Provides strong and accurate details to support the argument about the video
- Considers other perspectives on the purpose and effectiveness of the video
- Cites all sources used in the analysis

Organic Compounds

The element carbon is central to life. Over billions of years, chemicals that are derived from living things have built up in rocks. Over that time, these chemicals have been altered by heat and pressure, but their molecules are still based around carbon. As a result, all carbon compounds, including those produced in laboratories, are described as being organic. It is estimated that 90 percent of all compounds are organic. The main source is petroleum, which is a mixture of thousands of chemicals. Many of them contain just carbon and hydrogen, and so are called hydrocarbons. One carbon atom can bond with four other atoms. It can also form single, double, or triple covalent bonds with another carbon. Therefore, carbon atoms can produce a vast range of molecular shapes, including long chains and rings. The combinations of carbon atoms are almost endless, especially because organic compounds form **isomers**. Isomers are molecules that use the same number and type of atoms, but arrange them in different ways.

Aliphatic Compounds

Organic compounds based on chains of carbon atoms are known as aliphatic. The carbons are bonded to each other and the spare bonds connect to hydrogen atoms. Aliphatic compounds are mostly used as fuels.

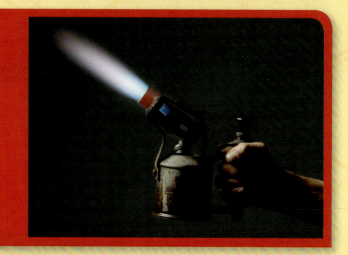

Aromatic Compounds

When carbon compounds contain a ring of six carbon atoms, they are aromatic. The simplest aromatic compound is benzene (C_6H_6). Aromatic compounds are highly stable and are used to make strong plastics.

With Oxygen

Many familiar organic compounds include oxygen atoms bonded to one or more of the carbons. They include alcohols, organic acids, such as vinegar, esters, which create food flavors, and aldehydes, often used in cosmetics.

Fossil Fuels

The petroleum industry extracts organic compounds from Earth and refines them into useful materials. Natural gas is made up of simple compounds, such as methane, while crude oil is a mixture of liquid and solid compounds.

Heterocyclic Compounds

Ringed organic compounds that include one or more non-carbon atoms, such as oxygen or sulfur, are termed heterocyclic. These compounds are used in many useful chemicals, such as dyes, explosives and medicines.

TEACHER NOTES

More

Organic Compounds
Review the different kinds of organic compounds.

1. Which hydrocarbons are the most reactive?
2. Describe the process of separating crude oil into different fractions in your own words.
3. What happens when a cyclic compound contains atoms other than carbon?

Video

How To Harden Vegetable Oils Through Hydrogenation
Learn how to harden vegetable oils through a chemical process demonstrated on the example of margarine.

1. What are the properties and consistency of margarine? How does this affect the amount of double bonds that are hydrogenated?
2. What is margarine an emulsion of? How does this affect its taste?

Chemistry

Polymers

The largest molecules of all, polymers are usually based on carbon and hydrogen, but often have other elements. Many natural products, such as wood and silk, are polymers. Polymers are built from smaller repeating units known as monomers. Some polymers, called homopolymers, contain just one monomer, but others, known as copolymers, are made up of two or more types of monomers. During polymerization, the monomers join up to make long chains. Although polymers can contain as few as five repeating units, most are made up of thousands or even millions. The material properties of a polymer can be tracked to the chemical activity of its monomers. Some polymers form strong crosslinks between monomers on different chains, creating a rigid substance. Weaker intermolecular forces between polymer chains make them tangle up, creating flexible and elastic materials.

Cellulose and starch

Cellulose and starch are the most common natural polymers. Both are made by plants and are based on the monomer glucose, a simple sugar. Starch is used by plants as a compact energy store. When sugar is needed, the starch is broken down into glucose molecules. Cellulose is the polymer that makes up the main structural material of plants. It is one of the most abundant organic substances on Earth, and cannot be readily broken down. Herbivorous animals that depend on eating cellulose have to rely on bacteria living in the gut to digest cellulose and release its sugars.

Rubber

Natural polymers are everywhere—in fact, many of them grow on or in trees. The sap from rubber trees provided the raw material for the earliest polymer industry.

Natural rubber, or latex, known to chemists as polyisoprene, is a polymer made up of monomers of isoprene (C_5H_8), which is in the sap. Isoprene contains two double bonds separated by a single bond. When it polymerizes, these bonds are broken and rearranged to allow the monomers to link up in a long, coiled chain.

Rubber is elastic because stretching tends to straighten out the entangled chains, but when the stretching force is released, the intermolecular forces pull the chains back together. Rubber polymers are hydrophobic, which means the molecules will not mix with

Liquid latex, a milky sap, coagulates into a stretchy solid when left in the air.

26 | 21st Century Science

water molecules and push them away. The opposite behavior is called hydrophilic. This makes rubber a waterproof material, which was its primary use.

Vulcanization

Natural rubber gets soft when hot, but this is solved by vulcanization, which links the long chains of polyisoprene together with sulfur bonds. The cross-links make the rubber tough even when hot by locking it into a permanent shape. Vulcanized rubber is used in tires. The addition of sulfur eventually degrades the rubber, as the sulfur bridges are steadily removed by reactions with oxygen in the air. Natural rubber has been largely replaced with a synthetic form made from petroleum that has stronger cross-linkages.

Synthetic Polymers

As well as making use of natural polymers, chemists began to imitate nature and build synthetic polymers. Plastics are polymers made using monomers derived mostly from petroleum and are used worldwide. Synthetic rubbers and artificial fabrics, such as nylon, are also made this way. However, in the 1800s, chemists sought synthetic alternatives to wood, silk, and resins, which are used in paints and varnishes. The first successful synthetic polymers were based on cellulose. They included silk-like fabrics such as rayon, but most have been superseded by petroleum-based products.

TEACHER NOTES

More
Synthetic Polymers
Review more about rayon, synthetic rubber, nylon, polyesters, and aramids.

1. What is rayon made from? How has it been made safer?
2. Compare and contrast synthetic rubber with natural latex. What advantages does each have? Are there any disadvantages?
3. What was the first completely synthetic fiber? Name its characteristics.

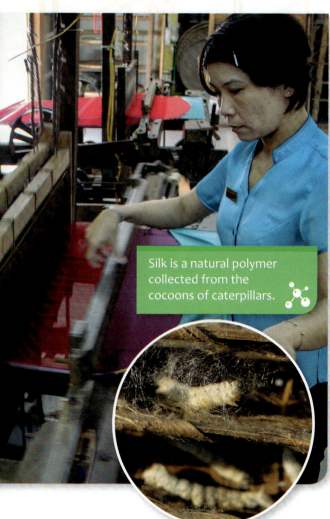

Silk is a natural polymer collected from the cocoons of caterpillars.

Vulcanized rubbers, like those used in tires, were invented by Charles Goodyear in 1844.

The term "plastic" originally described a substance that could be shaped easily.

Plastics

Nearly 4 percent of petroleum oil is used as a raw material for plastics. The naphtha, a mix of compounds containing between 8 to 12 carbon atoms, is extracted and "cracked," into smaller molecules. One of the products is ethene (C_2H_2)—the single most important substance for producing plastics, most notably polythene, which is used for plastic bags and bottles. The most common of all plastics is polyvinyl chloride (PVC). This tough material is used to make DVDs, waterproof clothing, the interior trim of cars, and is used to insulate electric cables. When one of the hydrogens in ethene is replaced by chlorine, the result is chloroethene, or vinyl chloride, the monomer at the heart of PVC.

Two kinds of plastic

Polythene, polystyrene, which makes styrofoam, PVC, and nylon are all thermoplastics. They are made up of tangled chains. Weak intermolecular forces hold the chains together and are removed by heat. The plastics soften on warming as the chains move over each other more easily. This is why thermoplastic polymers melt without changing their chemical structure and can be reshaped.

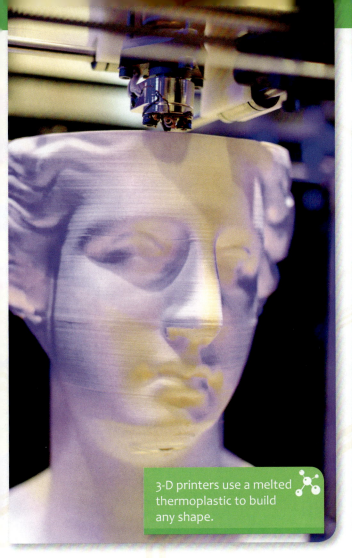

3-D printers use a melted thermoplastic to build any shape.

Shaping Plastics

Plastics and polymers are highly adaptable materials. They can be processed in different ways to provide a wide variety of shapes and structures. For example, nylon can be molded to make stiff syringes or flexible eyeglass frames, or it can be drawn into fibers to make anything from thin pantyhose to guitar strings. The many processes used to shape plastics include cold drawing, extrusion, injection molding, calendaring, and foaming. All can transform the same polymer into different materials.

By contrast, thermosetting polymers, such as Bakelite, formica, melamine and other methanal-based polymers have cross-linked chains. Strong covalent bonds both within and between the chains form a rigid three-dimensional network. The bonds form due to "curing" with heat or chemicals after the polymers have been shaped. Once the bonds have formed, the shape cannot be changed, and the plastic burns before it melts.

Adapting properties

A wide range of properties can be designed into plastics, with the result that these polymers are in use almost everywhere. Tough plastics are even able to replace ceramics and cast iron. The length of a chain and the amount of branching in it affects the physical properties of a polymer. Increasing the length of the polymer chain tends to produce stronger materials because longer chains tangle more easily and thus have more points of contact with neighboring chains. This leads to a greater number of attractive forces between molecules that hold the chains together. Straight chains can pack together more closely to form high-density polymers that are strong, but not very flexible, and that soften at relatively high temperatures. Polymers made of highly branched chains that cannot pack together very closely tend to be less dense, and may be glassy and transparent.

TEACHER NOTES

More
Shaping Plastics
Review drawing and extrusion, injection molding, blow molding, calendering, and foaming.

1. What characteristics are produced by cold drawing?
2. Which method is used to make hollow objects? Explain how in your own words.
3. Describe the process of foaming. What are the advantages of using this method?

Weblink
Conflicts in Chemistry: The Case of Plastics
Explore the science of plastics.

1. What are the two ways in which monomers can be chemically joined together? Describe the steps in your own words.
2. Why are amorphous polymers often used as food wrap or contact lenses?
3. What are the four general properties of polymers?

Chemistry 29

EXTENSION ACTIVITY

Analyzing a Scientific Blog

Students will complete a thorough analysis of a blog that explores scientific topics or events. An exemplary analysis will meet the following criteria.

- Chooses a relevant and meaningful blog
- Provides a working link to the blog
- Identifies the blogger
- Presents information about the blogger
- Assesses the blogger's reliability
- Considers and assesses the blogger's perspective
- Determines the blogger's intended audience
- Determines whether the blogger had first hand knowledge of the topic or event, or whether he or she is reporting as a secondary source
- Summarizes the topic or event that the blogger is covering
- Determines any bias present in the blog postings
- Examines and evaluates any content tags used by the blogger
- Uses additional sources to confirm any claims made by the blog
- Uses correct spelling, grammar, and punctuation

Vital Raw Materials

Different foods contain a range of raw materials needed by animals.

The study of the chemical reactions in living things is called biochemistry. Chemical reactions go on continuously in all organisms. When they cease, the organism dies. Living things of all kinds are largely made from molecules composed of just a handful of chemical elements. These are hydrogen, oxygen, carbon, nitrogen, phosphorus, and sulfur. Many other elements, most notably sodium and potassium, also perform vital roles, but are present in minute amounts. Food provides the essential raw materials and the energy needed to drive the reactions of life. Before any of the chemicals in food can be used by the body, the food must be broken down. Food is physically broken down by chewing and by churning in the stomach, and chemically broken up by enzymes—proteins that act as catalysts in living systems.

Respiration

Respiration is a complex sequence of chemical reactions in which sugars are broken down releasing their chemical energy in reactions with oxygen. As with combustion, the products of respiration are energy, carbon dioxide, and water. Some of the energy is released as heat, but most is captured in adenosine triphosphate (ATP) molecules. These are used elsewhere in the cell, where they break down into adenosine diphosphate (ADP) to release energy for use elsewhere in the cell.

Essential nutrients

In order to stay healthy, people must include in their diet **vitamins**, minerals, fiber, water, lipids which are fats and oils, carbohydrates, and proteins. The body can manufacture particular proteins, lipids, and carbohydrates from raw materials in foods. However, it cannot make vitamins or minerals, and these chemicals have roles in metabolism, the name given to all the biochemical reactions that work together to keep the organism alive. Fiber is indigestible cellulose, and it gives structure to foods and waste materials in the gut, keeping it healthy. Water, which makes up roughly 75 percent of the human body, provides the essential solvent in which biochemical processes take place.

Lipids and carbohydrates

Lipids have many roles in metabolism, such as acting as energy stores. Lipids comprise a glycerol molecule with three long fatty acid chains attached—all are hydrocarbons. The glycerol and fatty acids are released during digestion, and recombine as new fats in body tissues.

Carbohydrates, such as starches and sugars, are made up of carbon, hydrogen, and oxygen. These large molecules are broken down to form smaller sugars, which are the body's energy source.

Proteins

Proteins are polymers of amino acids—smaller molecules that include an amino group ($-NH_2$) and a carboxylic acid ($-COOH$). There are about 20 amino acids, which are combined in specific orders in huge numbers—up to 4,000 at a time—to make up thousands of unique proteins. The proteins in food are digested into amino acids, which are then used to build new proteins.

Glycolysis and the Krebs Cycle

Respiration involves two main phases, glycolysis and the Krebs, or citric acid, cycle. During glycolysis, glucose is broken into molecules of pyruvic acid. That requires energy from ATP to get started, but ends up releasing more energy than it uses—it is an exothermic reaction. The pyruvic acid then feeds into the Krebs cycle, which creates more ATP. ATP is the energy currency of the cell. The energy from respiration adds a phosphate group to an ADP, making ATP. When the cell needs that energy, ATP releases it by dropping the third phosphate.

TEACHER NOTES

▶ Video

Cellular Respiration Steps and Pathways
Learn more about aerobic and anaerobic cellular respiration by watching this video.

1. What happens during glycolysis? What is produced from this process?
2. Compare and contrast aerobic and anaerobic cellular respiration. How are they similar? In what ways are they different?

🌐 Weblink

Why do we Need Fats, Carbohydrates, and Proteins in our Diet?
Examine the blog post by Patrick Brown, a PhD candidate in the Biomedical Sciences Program at Penn State College of Medicine.

1. Who is the intended audience for this blog post? Is the tone and language used appropriate for this audience? Why or why not?
2. What are the writer's goals and how does he attempt to accomplish them? How successful is he? Why do you think so?
3. Why are fats essential for life? What is the body's primary source of energy?

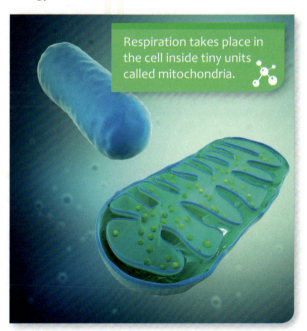

Respiration takes place in the cell inside tiny units called mitochondria.

During exercise, more energy is needed, and so more carbon dioxide is released and breathed out.

Chemistry | 31

Living Chemistry

All living things are chemical machines. Chemical reactions within the body provide **organisms** with energy, get rid of waste products, and keep them healthy. Almost all biological processes rely on catalysts in the form of proteins known as enzymes.

Enzymes

Enzymes are highly specialized proteins that regulate metabolism, the thousands of chemical processes that occur in a cell or organism. They act as organic catalysts that speed up chemical reactions in living cells. Without their catalyzing power, many biochemical reactions would proceed too slowly to sustain life. There are thousands of different enzymes in every single cell. Most work during metabolism as part of a chain reaction, or catalytic cycle. In general, the product of one enzyme-induced reaction becomes the reactant for the next.

The action of an enzyme is very specific. Most enzymes are involved in just one chemical reaction. Their structure explains why. Like all proteins, they are composed of chains of amino acids. This protein chain folds itself into a specific shape, which is held together by weak dipole forces and hydrogen bonds between amino acids. The surface of the enzyme contains specially shaped areas called active sites, in which the catalysis takes place. An enzyme's active site is precisely shaped to fit the reactants—known as the substrate in biochemistry—for a particular reaction. The process is called the "lock and key mechanism" in reference to the way that a lock is designed to accept only a particular key.

An enzyme becomes inactive if its shape is changed. This inactivation process is called denaturation. An enzyme may be denatured by changes in temperature, which cause the molecules to vibrate more vigorously and thus break the weak bonds that hold the chain in shape. Changes in pH can interfere with the ionic interactions within the protein chain, and this can also denature the enzyme.

Hormones

Hormones are the chemical messengers used by animals, including humans, to control and regulate body activity, such as growth and energy usage. In plants, phytohormones do a similar job. Hormones are produced in one part of the body, and then transported—usually via the bloodstream—to a target cell in another part, where they act by regulating preexisting processes.

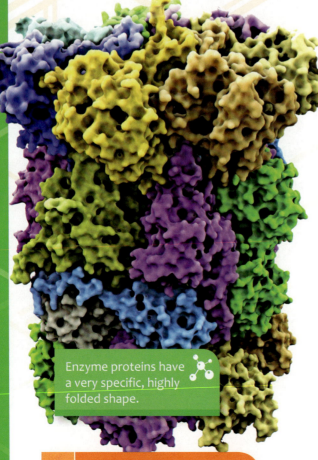

Enzyme proteins have a very specific, highly folded shape.

There are three main types of hormones. Peptide, polypeptide, and protein hormones such as somatotropin, the growth hormone, are formed from chains of amino acids of various lengths. Hormones such as epinephrine, also called adrenaline, which prepares the body for fast action in an emergency, are based on amino acid derivatives known as amides. These are organic compounds in which one or more of the hydrogen atoms in ammonia (NH_3) have been replaced by an acyl group (–RCO). Steroid hormones, such as the sex hormones, are based on the linked benzene rings that make up the molecule cholesterol.

Hormone actions

Hormones perform crucial roles. For example, the polypeptide hormones insulin and glucagon, and the amide-based hormone epinephrine, work together to control glucose levels in the blood. Glucose is stored, mainly in the liver and muscles, as the carbohydrate polymer glycogen. When blood glucose levels fall below normal, glucagon and epinephrine are released into the bloodstream. They act to increase the rate at which glycogen is converted to glucose. This leads to an increase in blood glucose levels.

If blood glucose levels become too high, insulin is released. It stimulates the liver and muscles to convert blood glucose into glycogen, so that glucose levels fall. In this feedback loop, the amounts of insulin and glucagon produced are determined by the level of glucose in the blood, while the overall level of glucose is determined by the balance between these two hormones.

Diabetic people do not produce enough insulin, and so are unable to take in glucose from their blood. Diabetes has many serious symptoms and can lead to death if not treated.

TEACHER NOTES

Transparency
The Lock and Key Mechanism
Examine the diagram and research online to learn more about the lock and key mechanism.

1. Explain what is happening in the diagram in your own words.
2. How is the lock and key model different from the induced fit model? Which is more accurate? Why?

Weblink
Mechanisms of Hormone Action
Review the article to learn more about the mechanisms of hormone action.

1. What functions do hormones serve?
2. What are the six steps of hormonal signaling?

The Lock and Key Mechanism

The substrate can only be changed when it is locked with the enzyme.

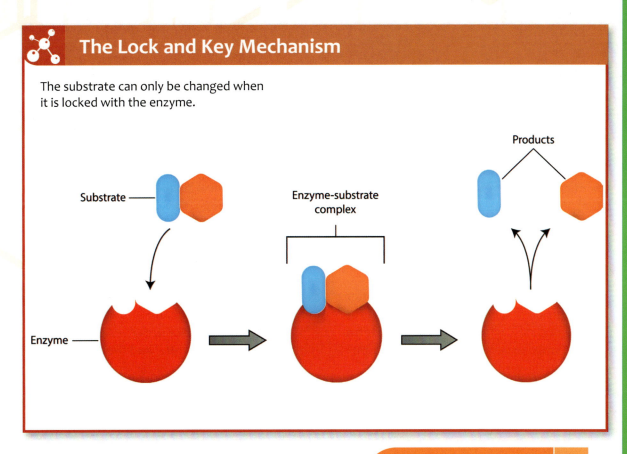

Chemistry

EXTENSION ACTIVITY

Analyzing a Primary Source

Students will complete a thorough analysis of a primary source. An exemplary analysis will meet the following criteria.

- Identifies the creator of the source
- Explains what medium was used to create the primary source
- Describes why the source qualifies as a primary one
- Explores any literary devices used in the source
- Identifies the intended audience for the source
- Relates the creator's goals in creating the source
- Illustrates knowledge of the period and location in which the source was created
- Distinguishes between facts and opinions found in the source
- Examines the reliability of the source's creator
- Compares the source with similar documents
- Cites additional sources used in the analysis
- Presents information in a clear, concise manner
- Uses correct spelling, grammar, and punctuation

Chemical plants run 24 hours a day to maximize efficiencies.

The Chemical Industry

The chemical industry works to transform raw materials such as oil, gas, coal, minerals, air, and water cheaply and efficiently into chemicals that can be used in the manufacture of other things. At a chemical plant, the reactants—or feedstock—are combined under appropriate conditions to produce the desired product.

Reaction conditions

It is important to find ways to make reactions occur quickly and efficiently. The focus is on the reaction rate, which is measured in terms of the change in concentration of a reactant or a product over time. Higher rates are achieved by increasing the concentration of the reactants, increasing contact between reactants by breaking them into smaller particles that are easier to mix. Increasing temperatures and pressures also speeds up a reaction, but industrial processes will use catalysts wherever possible to reduce the activation energies and obtain the optimum **yield**.

The optimum yield is not necessarily the maximum yield that can be achieved. When designing a plant, chemical engineers must consider the costs of maintaining the high pressures and temperatures needed to maximize a reaction rate, and the fact that fast exothermic reactions can be very difficult to control. The optimum reaction conditions balance cost and safety with yield.

Lithium salts used as feedstock are collected from desert salt lakes.

The Haber Process

The Haber process combines nitrogen gas (N_2) with hydrogen (H_2) to make ammonia (NH_3). It is named after Fritz Haber, the German chemist who devised it in 1909. Ammonia is the raw material used to make fertilizers, explosives, acids, and many other industrial chemicals that require nitrogen, such as dyes and drugs. Nitrogen derived from air is mixed with hydrogen made from natural gas (methane, CH_4). The hot, compressed gases pass over an iron catalyst where they react. The ammonia is cooled into a liquid, and any unreacted hydrogen and nitrogen is fed back into the system. The Haber process runs most efficiently at 752°F (400°C) and 250 atmospheres of pressure.

Processing options

Chemical engineers also determine which type of processing to use. In a batch process, raw materials are put into a vessel and allowed to react. When the reaction is complete, the product is removed and new feedstock is added for the next batch. In a continuous process, feedstock is constantly fed into the plant, and product flows out.

Batch processes are useful for slow reactions that produce relatively small amounts of product. Pharmaceutical products and food additives are typically manufactured in this way. They are also useful for manufacturing products that may explode or become contaminated. Continuous processes are more efficient for making vast quantities of product. For example, the most important industrial chemicals such as ammonia, chlorine, and acids are manufactured in this way. However, continuous processes require tailor-made plants, which are expensive to set up.

Waste and pollution

Waste is an inevitable product of all chemical plants, and plants are designed to manage it safely. In the past, operators tended to favor the "dilution solution"—dumping waste into the air or rivers and ocean, with the hope that it would become sufficiently diluted so as not to be harmful. Now, waste is contained in purpose-built ponds or heaps before being made safe. However, the waste can contaminate the land, or leak into groundwater or rivers. Chemical manufacturers are constantly developing chemical and mechanical waste treatment methods to meet the tougher legal requirements for waste disposal.

TEACHER NOTES

👁 First Hand
Letters Between Fritz Haber and Carl Bosch
Analyze the June 1933 correspondence between German chemists Fritz Haber and Carl Bosch.

1. What tone is used in each letter? Do you believe the writers are being sincere? Why or why not?
2. Why do you think Haber decided to leave Germany and accept an invitation from Cambridge, England?
3. Do you think Haber believed that Bosch had supported him sufficiently? Explain your answer.

📄 Document
The synthesis of ammonia from its elements
Review Fritz Haber's Nobel Lecture from June 2, 1920.

1. What arguments does Haber make? How does he support these arguments?
2. How do you think Haber's lecture was received at the time it was given? How might this lecture be viewed by scientists today?
3. Haber concludes his lecture, "It may be that this solution is not the final one...Let it suffice that in the meantime improved nitrogen fertilization of the soil brings new nutritive riches to mankind and that the chemical industry comes to the aid of the farmer who, in the good earth, changes stones into bread." What do you think Haber meant by this conclusion? From today's perspective, do you consider this solution to have been "final"? Why or why not?

Chemistry | 35

Medical Drugs

Diseases can result from an infection by a pathogen, a disease-causing agent, toxins from the environment, or from a malfunctioning of the body's own processes. Drugs are chemicals that tackle disease. They may attack the pathogens, remove toxins, or attempt to block or reverse the effects of the disease on the body, reducing symptoms and removing the problem. Vaccines are drugs that protect against illness by stimulating the body's immune system to develop defenses before being exposed to the pathogen. Most do this by making antibodies, which are proteins and other chemicals used by the body's defenses to target specific cells in the body, such as disease-causing organisms.

Antibiotics

Antibiotics are drugs that kill invading bacteria but do not damage the body's own cells. The first antibiotic was penicillin, which was first identified in the chemicals made by a mold, or fungi. It stops the growth of new bacteria by inhibiting the action of an enzyme responsible for making the bacteria's cell walls.

Drug mechanisms

Like enzymes, drugs depend on a "lock and key" mechanism to work. The drug molecule must fit exactly into a receptor on the molecule whose chemistry it hopes to influence. It is also critical that the drug is delivered efficiently to the part of the body it is supposed to affect. For example, a pill must be designed so that the drug can reach its target area when absorbed from the digestive system. In some cases, it is possible to attach a drug to an antibody, allowing the drug to target diseased cells directly. This approach is used to treat cancerous tumors, for example.

Finding new drugs

Many common drugs are derived from other organisms, mostly plants. For example, the painkiller aspirin is based on salicylic acid found in the bark of the willow tree. Drug researchers study chemicals from all kinds of plants—most often from tropical rainforests, where many new

Antibiotic tests prove that bacteria cannot grow in its presence.

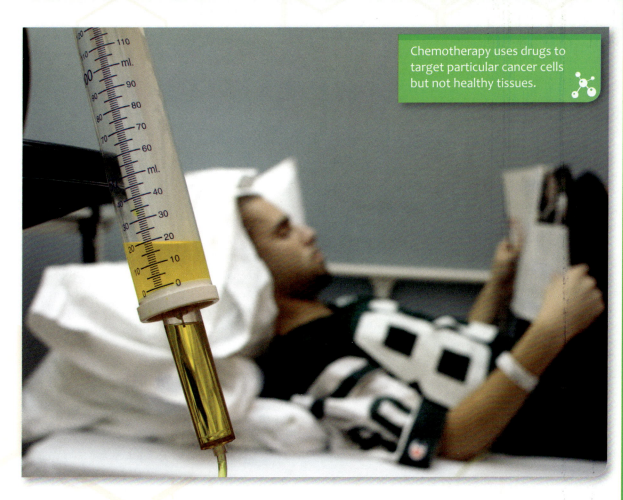

Chemotherapy uses drugs to target particular cancer cells but not healthy tissues.

species are being discovered. Drug companies ask local people for help in identifying plants that may have medicinal effects. **Venoms** are another interesting source of drugs. For example, the venom of the Brazilian arrowhead viper blocks an enzyme that raises blood pressure. By using the structure of the venom proteins as a starting point, chemists were able to synthesize a new drug called Captopril, which is used to lower blood pressure.

Chirality

Chemists consider the shape and orientation of a drug. Many biological molecules are chiral—they exist in right- and left-handed forms, or isomers. Although they have the same physical properties, the two forms have different effects on the body. In the case of the drug thalidomide, used in the 1950s, one isomer was a sedative that stopped people from feeling sick, but when taken by pregnant women, the other isomer caused the limbs of their unborn children to stop growing properly.

Testing a new drug

Medicinal chemists are beginning to use computers more to model the shape of the chemicals they want to target. The computer calculates how strong each bond is so the researchers can design a completely new drug molecule that will react with it and remove the problem. In spite of the increasing success of computer-based drug design, developing a safe drug is still very expensive. Only about 1 in 10,000 of the compounds synthesized get through the rigorous testing to become a commercial drug.

TEACHER NOTES

First Hand
Organic Chemistry in Drug Discovery
Review the article by Malcolm MacCoss and Thomas A. Baillie.

1. Who do you think is the intended audience for this source? Why?
2. What stance, if any, do the authors take on this issue?
3. What conclusions do MacCoss and Baillie draw? Do you agree or disagree? Support your answer.

Weblink
Stereochemistry: Determining Molecular Chirality
Examine the discussion of chiral and achiral objects.

1. Explain what the term "enantiomers" means in your own words.
2. How can you determine if a molecule is chiral using the superposability requirement?

Chemistry | 37

Chemistry in Food and Agriculture

Every year, the agriculture industry uses millions of tons (tonnes) of artificial fertilizers, which add nutrients essential for plant growth that have been used up by the previously crop. Farmers also use chemicals called pesticides to kill unwanted insects and weed plants.

Fertilizers

The main elements required by plants are phosphorus (P), potassium (K), and nitrogen (N). Phosphorus fertilizers are made from the mineral apatite and other naturally occurring phosphates compounds. Potassium fertilizers include three salts. These are potassium chloride, potassium nitrate, and potassium sulfates. Most modern nitrogen fertilizers are made from ammonia, produced by the Haber process, and can be applied to the land directly. Alternatively, the ammonia is made into salts such as ammonium sulfate and ammonium phosphate.

Dealing with pests

Farmers use herbicides for killing plants that are considered weeds. Selective weedkillers, which attack particular species, include diquat and paraquat. Systemic herbicides are applied to the soil, where they are picked up by the roots and distributed throughout the plant to kill it. Fungicides are used to kill damaging molds. Traditional fungicides included toxic compounds containing cadmium, copper, and mercury. Modern fungicides are synthetic organic compounds, which break down faster in the soil and so do not cause as much

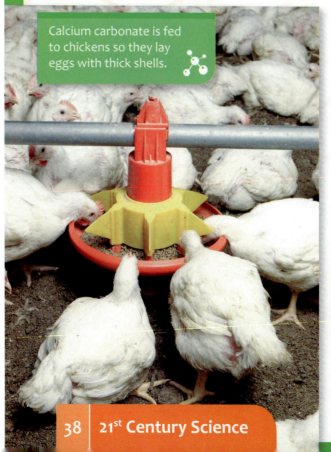

Calcium carbonate is fed to chickens so they lay eggs with thick shells.

Pesticides are toxic and must be used in a controlled manner.

pollution. Insecticides kill pests in two ways. Contact poisons go through the insect's body. They include natural substances, such as nicotine, and synthetic substances, such as organochlorine compounds. Dieldrin, dichlorodiphenyltrichloroethane (DDT), malathion, and parathion are examples of organochlorine compounds. Other insecticides poison the pests after they take them in with food. These include compounds containing arsenic or fluorine.

Pollution from agrochemicals

In Western nations, there has been increasing concern that chemicals applied to the land and crops can result in pollution of water supplies. This concern has prompted a growing interest in returning to organic farming methods. However, one in three people in the world rely on agricultural chemicals to provide them with food. Without them the global crop yield would not feed everyone, but farmers are learning to use fewer chemicals in a more efficient way.

Chemistry of Food

The purpose of farming is to produce food. Food is a supply of chemical energy and raw materials for maintaining the body.

Carbohydrates
Simple sugars are most common in sweet fruits, while cereal grains contain starches, which are complex carbohydrates.

Lipids
As fats and oils, lipids are found in both plant and animal foods. They are common in seeds, nuts, fish, milk, and meat.

Proteins
As well as being used as enzymes, proteins are also used in animal muscle. As well as meat, proteins are in eggs and nuts.

Vitamins and Minerals
These are essential chemicals that the body cannot build itself. The body needs a small but constant supply, which is best achieved by eating a varied diet.

TEACHER NOTES

Transparency
Chemistry of Food
Examine the diagram and research online to learn more about carbohydrates, lipids, proteins, vitamins, and minerals.

1. Describe the structure/function relationships in food molecules.
2. What are the effects of processing, fortification, and packaging on the nutritional quality of foods?

Document
Agrochemical-Related Environmental Pollution: Effects on Human Health
Analyze the article from the *Global Journal of Biology, Agriculture & Health Sciences*.

1. What is the goal of this article? Is it successful in achieving this goal? How are the main points of this article presented?
2. The article claims that, "To prevent environmental pollution and occupational diseases, proactive preventative actions are needed, including preserving the environment and enforcing appropriate laws." Do you agree with this assertion? Why or why not?

Chemistry | 39

Chemistry in Nature

Many of the processes of the natural world are driven by chemical reactions. For example, life on Earth is sustained by a set of chemical reactions called photosynthesis. Plants, algae, and certain bacteria all use photosynthesis to capture energy radiated from the Sun and use that to make sugar fuel. That sugar is also the primary source of energy for all animals, fungi, and non-photosynthetic lifeforms.

Biological pigments

Photosynthesis is a photochemical reaction. The key molecules in all light-driven biochemical process are pigments, which capture the energy of light. Incoming photons boost the energy of electrons in some of the pigment's atoms. The pigment in photosynthesis is chlorophyll, a molecule with four benzene rings surrounding a magnesium ion (Mg^{2+}). A similar pigment is hemoglobin, which makes blood cells red and has the job of carrying oxygen around the body. Instead of magnesium, a hemoglobin molecule contains an iron ion (Fe^{2+}). Chlorophyll takes in light energy in the red and blue region of the visible spectrum. It reflects back the green light.

Light and dark reactions

Photosynthesis involves three series of chemical events—the light reactions and the dark reactions, during which energy is captured and stored, and a series of reactions to replenish the pigments. The light reactions can take place only in the presence of light, and occur inside chloroplasts—tiny green units that are inside most plants cells. During the reactions, a photon of light is captured by the chlorophyll molecule and excites an electron within the pigment. The excited electron causes a protein pump to release a proton. The proton's energy is then captured by an ATP. In addition, a second type of energy-carrying molecule, nicotine adenine dinucleotide phosphate (NADP), is reduced to form the electron carrier NADPH.

Magnesium ions in chlorophyll make the natural world green.

During the dark reactions, the energy from ATP and NADPH is used to convert carbon dioxide and water into more complex organic compounds, eventually forming glucose ($C_6H_{12}O_6$). During the third series of reactions, the electron that was stripped from the chlorophyll at the beginning of the light reactions is replaced.

Atmospheric Chemistry

Earth has a chemically reactive atmosphere, rich in pure oxygen. The chemistry of the atmosphere is a series of delicately balanced cycles involving many chemicals that interact closely. Without the atmosphere, the surface of Earth would have an average temperature of about 0°F (–18°C). The greenhouse effect traps some of the energy of the Sun, raising the surface to a more comfortable 59°F (15°C). This occurs because the "greenhouse gases," mainly water vapor, methane, and carbon dioxide, trap the heat radiating from the ground, warming the lower part of the atmosphere, called the troposphere. The troposphere is where weather systems form as air masses of different temperatures and pressures mix to create winds and storms. Burning hydrocarbon fuels raises the levels of CO_2 to unnatural levels and makes the troposphere warmer.

TEACHER NOTES

🌐 **Weblink**

Atmospheric Chemistry
Review the article about atmospheric chemistry.

1. How do atmospheric scientists view the atmosphere?
2. What gases are pollutants in the atmosphere?

Increasing greenhouse gases are making weather more extreme.

Chemistry | 41

EXTENSION ACTIVITY

Answer a Scientific Question

Students will define a scientific question or problem, and carry out an investigation or experiment to answer it, then write a report on their findings. An exemplary report will meet the following criteria.

- Problem is written in the form of a question with a question mark at the end
- Hypothesis is written as a guess or explanation to the answer of the problem
- Hypothesis is written in a complete sentence (for example, "I think ...," "I hypothesize ...,""If..., then...")
- Variable and controls are clearly identified
- Procedure steps are in numbered order
- Procedure steps show what to measure and where to record the data
- Procedure steps are written in complete sentences
- Data is organized in a data table
- The investigation or experiment includes more then one trial
- All numbers have labels
- All calculations are complete
- Conclusion is written in complete sentences
- Conclusion states whether the hypothesis was right or wrong
- Conclusion answers the question written in the problem

Even the steam, or hot water vapor, produced by industry can be polluting.

A Cleaner Environment

Human use of chemicals inevitably leads to pollution. Some pollutants are synthetic chemicals, including powerful pesticides such as DDT, which have never existed in nature, and poison wildlife and damage plant life. Once these chemicals are shown to be harmful, they are invariably removed from use or are heavily controlled. Other pollutants are naturally occurring chemicals, which have been released into the environment in huge, unnatural amounts, and disrupt the balance of natural chemical reactions. Such chemicals include nitrogen oxides from car exhausts, sulfur-rich gases from industry, and carbon dioxide from burning hydrocarbon fuels, such as coal, gasoline, and natural gas. Humans are very reliant on these chemicals and so controlling their polluting effects is much more difficult.

What is pollution?

Pollution is anything that is found in the environment in unnatural amounts. Heat, light, and sound can be pollution in many habitats. More obvious examples are waste products of industry that are released into the air and water. Plastic trash does not decay or corrode in the same way as food waste or discarded iron and copper items. Over several decades, plastic particles have built up in all parts of the biosphere, the region of Earth where life exists. Plastics are even found in deep sea sediments and will one day become a components of rocks—making an entirely new type of stone. The solution to this is to use less plastic items, especially disposable bags and bottles, to recycle plastic items whenever possible, and to make use of plastics that can be decomposed by fungi and bacteria.

Using chemistry

As well as cutting back on producing polluting materials, chemistry can be used to solve the problem. Since the late 1980s, all cars have been fitted with catalytic converters. The car's exhaust passes through the "cat", where its gases meet metallic catalysts such as platinum, iridium, and rhodium. These convert the toxic gases in the exhaust into safer alternatives. Carbon monoxide, unburned hydrocarbons, and nitrogen oxides become carbon dioxide, water, and nitrogen. Similar "scrubber" systems clean the emissions from chemical factories and power plants.

Acid Rain

Issue
Sulfur oxides in the air react with water to form acids. These fall as rain, killing plants and changing the pH of soil and water.

Solution
Sulfur oxides are largely produced by burning coal. Sulfur is a common impurity in this fuel. The sulfur oxides must be removed from the smoke using chemical scrubbers.

Climate Change

Issue
Carbon dioxide and methane trap extra heat in the atmosphere, creating more extreme weather, such as longer droughts and more violent storms.

Solution
Burning hydrocarbon fuels releases an unnatural amount of carbon dioxide. Replacing these fuels with cleaner wind and solar power reduces emissions of greenhouse gases.

Smog

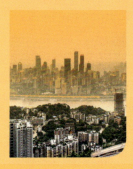

Issue
Dense clouds of smoke, dust particles, and water vapor form over large cities, increasing lung diseases and breathing problems.

Solution
Smog is strongly linked to gases and dust particles released by gasoline and diesel vehicles. The use of electric cars reduces the emissions of these exhaust gases.

Water Pollution

Issue
Aquatic wildlife is very sensitive to pollution. Fertilizers washed into rivers and lakes also make water plants grow more quickly than is natural.

Solution
Water pollution is due to chemical waste, sewage, and hot water from industrial plants. Water quality must be tested regularly and sources of pollution identified.

TEACHER NOTES

Weblink
Acid Rain
Review the article to discover more about acid rain.

1. What is acid rain? What causes acid rain?
2. Compare and contrast wet deposition and dry deposition.
3. How is acid rain measured?

EXTENSION ACTIVITY

Creating a Timeline

Students will explore a topic related to a scientific event and create a timeline to present their research on scientific events connected to this topic. An exemplary timeline will meet the following criteria.

- Includes the most significant events pertaining to the topic to be compared and analyzed
- Includes interesting events
- Uses accurate information for all events, including date, location, and major details
- Orders the events in a
- chronological sequence
- Describes each event with accurate, vivid, and specific details
- Presents the topic from three or more perspectives
- Inspires the reader to ask thoughtful questions regarding the events and perspectives presented in the timeline
- Uses correct spelling, grammar, and punctuation
- Presents the timeline in a visually attractive and striking manner
- Presents the timeline in a neat, organized manner that is logical and easy to follow
- Uses creativity to present the timeline in an engaging manner
- Effectively communicates historical information relating to the topic
- Supports each event with reliable sources
- Includes a correctly formatted bibliography of all sources used to create the timeline

Timeline of Innovations in Chemistry

440 BC Democritus suggests that matter is made from indivisible particles called atoms. He proposes that atoms have different shapes, which makes them cling together to make solids or slide past each other to make liquids.

1754 Joseph Black discovers carbon dioxide gas, calling it "fixed air." This is the first evidence that air is made from a mixture of separate gases.

▼ **1778** Antoine Lavoisier shows that water is made by reacting oxygen and hydrogen. Before that, it had been assumed that water was an element in its own right.

1828 Friedrich Wöhler shows that living things depend upon chemical processes. Before that, it is thought that living things are powered by a mysterious force that is separate to other kinds of chemistry.

▼ **1897** J. J. Thomson discovers the electron in a beam produced by a strong electric current inside a vacuum tube.

1911 Ernest Rutherford discovers that atoms have a positively charged nucleus at their center. He later reveals that the nucleus contains particles, which he names protons.

1913 Henry Moseley finds that atoms have a specific "atomic number" of protons. Each element has its own specific number.

1932 James Chadwick discovers the neutron.

1995 Eric Cornell and Carl Wieman cool rubidium to −459.7°F (−273.1°C) so its atoms merge together into a strange state of matter called the Bose-Einstein condensate.

2011 Daniel Schectman wins the Nobel Prize for creating quasicrystals, which are tiny units of metal that have a form unseen in naturally occurring chemicals.

Quiz

1. What kind of electron microscope can detect a single atom?

2. Which type of bond involves electrons moving from one atom to another?

3. What is the name of a substance that lowers the activation energy of a chemical reaction?

4. What does pH stand for when chemists measure the strength of an acid or base?

5. In an electrochemical cell, is the anode positively or negatively charged?

6. What is the name of the organic compounds that are based on a ring of six carbon atoms?

7. Of which kind of polymer is PVC an example?

8. What chemical is manufactured using the Contact process?

9. What does the acronym ATP stand for?

10. What metal atom in chlorophyll molecules makes it—and plant leaves—appear green?

Answers
1. Scanning tunneling microscope 2. Ionic bond 3. Catalysts 4. Potential hydrogen 5. Positively charged 6. Aromatic 7. A plastic 8. Sulfuric acid 9. Adenosine triphosphate 10. Magnesium

TEACHER NOTES

Transparency
Timeline of Innovations
Analyze important discoveries related to chemistry.

1. Why might these innovations be featured in the timeline? What makes these particular discoveries important?
2. How do you think the general public would have viewed these events when they first happened? How might their opinions have differed from those of scientists? Why? Give reasons for your answer.
3. What effect did these discoveries have on modern science?
4. How might these innovations have shaped the world today? What sources can be used to illustrate these effects?

Key Words

atom: the smallest unit of an element. Breaking an atom into smaller particles destroys it, so it does not represent an element anymore

atomic number: the number of protons in the nucleus of an element. Carbon, for instance, has 6 protons in its nucleus, and so its atomic number is 6

catalyst: a substance that promotes or accelerates a chemical reaction, without itself being permanently changed in the reaction

chemical reaction: an interaction between elements and compounds during which the atoms are rearranged, so transforming them to make new substances

dipole: a weak positive–negative polarity in a covalent molecule that is involved in weak bonds

electrode: a contact through which electricity enters a substance

electrolysis: the process in which a compound is split into its constituent elements, using an electric current

emulsion: a mixture where droplets of one liquid are suspended in another liquid

energy: the ability to do work, to move matter, or change its state. Chemical reactions are driven by energy

hydrocarbon: a chemical compound that is made up only of carbon and hydrogen atoms. Fossil fuels, such as oil and natural gas, are mostly made up of hydrocarbons

hydrogen bond: a weak bond formed between a polarized hydrogen atom and an electronegative atom, or one that attracts electrons, such as oxygen. Water is held together with these bonds

ion: an atom that is positively or negatively charged after it has lost or gained electrons

isomers: molecules that have the same formula, or the same numbers of the same atoms, but these atoms are arranged in different ways

noble gases: gases in Group VIII of the Periodic Table, all of which are chemically unreactive. Helium and neon are noble gases

nucleus: the central core of the atom, which is made of protons, and in most cases, neutrons

orbital: another name for the location of an electron in an atom. Electrons occupy a certain space, or shell, that moves around the nucleus

ore: a naturally occurring substance, generally found in rocks, that contains a valuable source of an element, mostly metals, such as gold or iron

organism: a living thing, such as an animal, plant, or bacteria

ozone layer: a thin layer in the upper atmosphere that is rich in a form of oxygen known as ozone. The ozone layer protects Earth from harmful ultraviolet and other radiation

reactants: elements or compounds taking part in a chemical reaction

solute: a solid or liquid dissolved in a solvent

solvent: a liquid in which certain solids or other liquids dissolve

venom: a poison made by a living thing that is injected into an animal. Venom is used for killing prey or for defense

vitamins: simple chemicals found in food that are essential in small amounts for correct body functioning

wavelength: the distance between the top of one wave crest and the next

yield: a percentage calculated as the amount of product compared to the amount of feedstock used to produce that product

Index

acid rain 43
acids 14, 15, 22, 25, 31, 32, 33, 35, 43
aliphatic compounds 24
aluminum 20, 21
antibiotics 36
aromatic compounds 24
atoms 4, 5, 6, 7, 8, 10, 11, 12, 13, 18, 19, 24, 25, 28, 33, 40, 44, 45, 46
ATP 30, 31, 40, 41, 45

base 13, 14, 15, 45
Bose-Einstein condensate 44

carbohydrates 30, 31, 39
carbon dioxide 11, 15, 16, 30, 31, 41, 42, 43, 44
catalyst 13, 22, 30, 34, 35, 42
chemical reaction 8, 12, 20, 32, 45, 46
chlorine 12, 18, 19, 20, 23, 28, 35
climate change 43
combustion 13, 16, 17, 30
copper 14, 21, 38, 42
covalent bond 11

Dalton, John 5, 6
dipole 11, 32
distillation 8, 9
drug 4, 36, 37

electrochemical reactions 20
electrode 20
electrolysis 20, 21, 23, 46
electron 4, 6, 7, 10, 11, 12, 14, 20, 21, 40, 41, 44, 45, 46
electroplating 20, 21
elements 4, 5, 7, 8, 10, 12, 13, 17, 24, 26, 30, 38, 44, 46
emulsion 9, 19
energy 8, 11, 12, 13, 16, 17, 18, 19, 26, 30, 31, 32, 39, 40, 41, 45, 46
enzymes 30, 32, 36, 39
explosives 17, 22, 25, 35

fertilizers 22, 35, 38

glucose 16, 26, 31, 33, 41
greenhouse gases 41, 43
gunpowder 4, 17

Haber process 35, 38
hemoglobin 40
hydrocarbons 17, 16, 24, 31, 41, 42, 43, 46
hydrochloric acid 14, 23
hydrogen 7, 8, 11, 13, 14, 15, 18, 19, 20, 24, 26, 30, 31, 32, 33, 35, 44, 45, 46
hydrogen bond 11

ionic bond 10, 11
isomers 24, 37

Lavoisier, Antoine 44
lipids 30, 39
lock and key mechanism 32, 36

magnesium 12, 40
mixtures 8, 9, 12, 17, 18, 20, 22, 23, 24, 25, 44, 46

natural gas 16, 17, 35, 42, 46
neutrons 4, 6, 7, 10, 46
noble gas 10
nucleus 5, 6, 7, 44, 46
nylon 4, 27, 28, 29

oxygen 7, 8, 11, 13, 15, 16, 17, 19, 20, 22, 25, 27, 30, 31, 40, 41, 44, 46
ozone layer 4, 19, 46

Periodic Table 5, 7, 46
petroleum 22, 24, 25, 27, 28
pH 15, 32, 43, 45
photography 18
photosynthesis 13, 18, 40
plastics 22, 24, 28, 29, 42
pollution 19, 35, 39, 42, 43
polymers 26, 27, 28, 29, 31

polyvinyl chloride 45
products 12, 13, 17, 20, 22, 23, 26, 27, 28, 30, 32, 35, 42
proteins 30, 31, 32, 36, 37, 39
protons 4, 6, 7, 10, 14, 40, 44, 46

reactants 12, 13, 17, 32, 34
Rutherford, Ernest 44

salt 9, 10, 11, 14, 15, 20, 35
silver 19
smog 43
sodium 11, 12, 14, 15, 20, 23, 30
solution 9, 20, 23, 35, 42
solvent 9, 31, 46
sugars 16, 26, 30, 31, 39
sulfur 13, 22, 23, 25, 27, 30, 42, 43
sulfuric acid 22, 23

Thomson, J. J. 44

vitamins 39, 46

water 8, 9, 10, 11, 13, 14, 15, 16, 20, 22, 23, 27, 30, 34, 39, 41, 42, 43, 44

LIGHTBOX

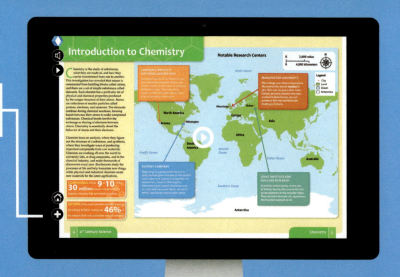

➕ SUPPLEMENTARY RESOURCES

Click on the plus icon ➕ found in the bottom left corner of each spread to open additional teacher resources.

- Download and print the book's quizzes and activities
- Access curriculum correlations
- Explore additional web applications that enhance the Lightbox experience

LIGHTBOX DIGITAL TITLES
Packed full of integrated media

VIDEOS

INTERACTIVE MAPS

WEBLINKS

SLIDESHOWS

QUIZZES

OPTIMIZED FOR
✓ TABLETS
✓ WHITEBOARDS
✓ COMPUTERS
✓ AND MUCH MORE!

Published by Smartbook Media Inc.
350 5th Avenue, 59th Floor New York, NY 10118
Website: www.openlightbox.com

Copyright © 2018 Smartbook Media Inc.
All rights reserved. No part of this publication may be reproduced, stored in a retrieval system, or transmitted in any form or by any means, electronic, mechanical, photocopying, recording, or otherwise, without the prior written permission of the publisher.

Library of Congress Control Number: 2017936626

ISBN 978-1-5105-1887-2 (hardcover)
ISBN 978-1-5105-1888-9 (multi-user eBook)

Printed in the United States of America in Brainerd, Minnesota
1 2 3 4 5 6 7 8 9 0 21 20 19 18 17

062017
050317

Editor: Katie Gillespie
Art Director: Terry Paulhus

Every reasonable effort has been made to trace ownership and to obtain permission to reprint copyright material. The publisher would be pleased to have any errors or omissions brought to its attention so that they may be corrected in subsequent printings. The publisher acknowledges Getty Images, Shutterstock, Dreamstime, and Alamy as its primary image suppliers for this title.